D0469615

100 GREATEST

WEDDING
POEMS

AND READINGS

Quarto Classics

Selected by Richard Happer

Published by Quarto Classics
An imprint of JonesCat Publishing Ltd
Edinburgh EH10 4LW

ISBN 9780956242891

'When you realize you want to spend the rest of your life with somebody, you want the rest of your life to start as soon as possible.'

From *When Harry Met Sally*, by Nora Ephron

'Whatever our souls are made of, his and mine are the same.'

Emily Brönte

'The groom always smiles proudly because he's convinced he's accomplished something quite wonderful. The bride smiles because she's been able to convince him of it.'

Judith McNaught

'If you live to be a hundred, I want to live to be a hundred minus one day so I never have to live without you.'

Winnie-the-Pooh, A. A. Milne

INTRODUCTION

It can be tricky to find the perfect words to celebrate your perfect day.

You may want a poem for your wedding to celebrate love, friendship, commitment, joy, family, togetherness or any one of a thousand other emotions in a few beautiful words – it's no easy task.

Luckily the world's greatest poets, whose business Love is, have found myriad wonderful ways to express the inexpressible.

Shakespeare, Tennyson, Dickinson, Donne, Yeats, Keats, Burns, Lawrence, Tennyson, Whitman, Byron, Shelley, Wordsworth, Rossetti, Donne and more – here are the very best of their most moving, yearning, happy and exciting odes to Love and Marriage.

We've included biblical and non-religious readings as well as poems. All the famous ones are in here (yes, including the reading from *Love, Actually*!), and many more little-known, fresh and quirky selections.

Which one will you choose for your perfect day? Which will be your partner's favourite?

Read them to each other and find out together...

CONTENTS

POEMS

HEARTS ON FIRE

MARRIAGE

HAPPILY EVER AFTER

READINGS

BIBLICAL

NON-RELIGIOUS

POEMS

HEARTS ON FIRE

I Will Make You Brooches
Robert Louis Stevenson

I will make you brooches and toys for your delight
Of bird-song at morning and star-shine at night.
I will make a palace fit for you and me
Of green days in forests and blue days at sea.

I will make my kitchen, and you shall keep your room,
Where white flows the river and bright blows the broom,
And you shall wash your linen and keep your body white
In rainfall at morning and dewfall at night.

And this shall be for music when no one else is near,
The fine song for singing, the rare song to hear!
That only I remember, that only you admire,
Of the broad road that stretches and the roadside fire.

How Do I Love Thee? Let Me Count The Ways.
Elizabeth Barrett Browning

How do I love thee? Let me count the ways.
I love thee to the depth and breadth and height
My soul can reach, when feeling out of sight
For the ends of being and ideal grace.
I love thee to the level of every day's
Most quiet need, by sun and candle-light.
I love thee freely, as men strive for right;
I love thee purely, as they turn from praise.
I love thee with the passion put to use
In my old griefs, and with my childhood's faith.
I love thee with a love I seemed to lose
With my lost saints. I love thee with the breath,
Smiles, tears, of all my life; and, if God choose,
I shall but love thee better after death.

Wild nights – Wild nights!
Emily Dickinson

Wild nights - Wild nights!
Were I with thee
Wild nights should be
Our luxury!

Futile - the winds -
To a Heart in port -
Done with the Compass -
Done with the Chart!

Rowing in Eden -
Ah - the Sea!
Might I but moor - tonight -
In thee!

To His Coy Mistress
Andrew Marvell

Had we but world enough and time,
This coyness, lady, were no crime.
We would sit down, and think which way
To walk, and pass our long love's day.
Thou by the Indian Ganges' side
Shouldst rubies find; I by the tide
Of Humber would complain. I would
Love you ten years before the flood,
And you should, if you please, refuse
Till the conversion of the Jews.
My vegetable love should grow
Vaster than empires and more slow;
An hundred years should go to praise
Thine eyes, and on thy forehead gaze;
Two hundred to adore each breast,
But thirty thousand to the rest;
An age at least to every part,
And the last age should show your heart.
For, lady, you deserve this state,
Nor would I love at lower rate.

     But at my back I always hear
Time's wingèd chariot hurrying near;
And yonder all before us lie
Deserts of vast eternity.
Thy beauty shall no more be found;
Nor, in thy marble vault, shall sound
My echoing song; then worms shall try

That long-preserved virginity,
And your quaint honour turn to dust,
And into ashes all my lust;
The grave's a fine and private place,
But none, I think, do there embrace.
     Now therefore, while the youthful hue
Sits on thy skin like morning dew,
And while thy willing soul transpires
At every pore with instant fires,
Now let us sport us while we may,
And now, like amorous birds of prey,
Rather at once our time devour
Than languish in his slow-chapped power.
Let us roll all our strength and all
Our sweetness up into one ball,
And tear our pleasures with rough strife
Through the iron gates of life:
Thus, though we cannot make our sun
Stand still, yet we will make him run.

Longing
Matthew Arnold

Come to me in my dreams, and then
By day I shall be well again!
For so the night will more than pay
The hopeless longings of the day.
Come, as thou cam'st a thousand times,
A messenger from radiant climes,
And smile on thy new world, and be
As kind to others as to me!
Or, as thou never cam'st in sooth,
Come now, and let me dream it truth,
And part my hair, and kiss my brow,
And say, My love! why sufferest thou?
Come to me in my dreams, and then
By day I shall be well again!
For so the night will more than pay
The hopeless longings of the day.

Meeting at Night
Robert Browning

I
The grey sea and the long black land;
And the yellow half-moon large and low;
And the startled little waves that leap
In fiery ringlets from their sleep,
As I gain the cove with pushing prow,
And quench its speed i' the slushy sand.

II
Then a mile of warm sea-scented beach;
Three fields to cross till a farm appears;
A tap at the pane, the quick sharp scratch
And blue spurt of a lighted match,
And a voice less loud, thro' its joys and fears,
Than the two hearts beating each to each!

Madonna of the Evening Flowers
Amy Lowell

All day long I have been working
Now I am tired.
I call: "Where are you?"
But there is only the oak tree rustling in the wind.
The house is very quiet,
The sun shines in on your books,
On your scissors and thimble just put down,
But you are not there.
Suddenly I am lonely:
Where are you?
I go about searching.

Then I see you,
Standing under a spire of pale blue larkspur,
With a basket of roses on your arm.
You are cool, like silver,
And you smile.
I think the Canterbury bells are playing little tunes,
You tell me that the peonies need spraying,
That the columbines have overrun all bounds,
That the pyrus japonica should be cut back and rounded.
You tell me these things.
But I look at you, heart of silver,
White heart-flame of polished silver,
Burning beneath the blue steeples of the larkspur,
And I long to kneel instantly at your feet,
While all about us peal the loud, sweet Te Deums of the
Canterbury bells.

Love Not Me
John Wilbye

Love not me for comely grace,
For my pleasing eye or face,
Nor for any outward part,
No, nor for a constant heart:
     For these may fail or turn to ill,
     So thou and I shall sever:
Keep, therefore, a true woman's eye,
And love me still but know not why--
     So hast thou the same reason still
     To doat upon me ever!

On a Girdle
Edmund Waller

That which her slender waist confin'd,
Shall now my joyful temples bind;
No monarch but would give his crown,
His arms might do what this has done.

It was my heaven's extremest sphere,
The pale which held that lovely deer,
My joy, my grief, my hope, my love,
Did all within this circle move.

A narrow compass, and yet there
Dwelt all that's good, and all that's fair;
Give me but what this ribbon bound,
Take all the rest the sun goes round.

Ah, God, the Way Your Little Finger Moved
Stephen Crane

Ah, God, the way your little finger moved,
As you thrust a bare arm backward
And made play with your hair
And a comb, a silly gilt comb
—Ah, God—that I should suffer
Because of the way a little finger moved.

On the Balcony
D.H. Lawrence

In front of
the sombre mountains,
a faint, lost ribbon of rainbow
And between us and it, the thunder;
And down below in the green wheat,
the labourers stand like dark stumps,
still in the green wheat.
You are near to me, and naked feet
In their sandals, and through the
scent of the balcony's naked timber
I distinguish the scent of your hair:
so now the limber
Lightning falls from heaven.
Adown the pale-green glacier river floats
A dark boat through the gloom —
and whither? The thunder roars
But still we have each other!
The naked lightnings in the heavens dither
And disappear —
what have we but each other?
The boat has gone.

Sonnet XVIII
William Shakespeare

Shall I compare thee to a summer's day?
Thou art more lovely and more temperate:
Rough winds do shake the darling buds of May,
And summer's lease hath all too short a date:
Sometime too hot the eye of heaven shines,
And often is his gold complexion dimm'd;
And every fair from fair sometime declines,
By chance, or nature's changing course, untrimm'd;
But thy eternal summer shall not fade
Nor lose possession of that fair thou ow'st;
Nor shall Death brag thou wander'st in his shade,
When in eternal lines to time thou grow'st;
So long as men can breathe or eyes can see,
So long lives this, and this gives life to thee.

The Bracelet: To Julia
Robert Herrick

Why I tie about thy wrist,
Julia, this silken twist;
For what other reason is 't
But to show thee how, in part,
Thou my pretty captive art?
But thy bond-slave is my heart:
'Tis but silk that bindeth thee,
Knap the thread and thou art free;
But 'tis otherwise with me:
—I am bound and fast bound, so
That from thee I cannot go;
If I could, I would not so.

The Indian Serenade
Percy Bysshe Shelley

I arise from dreams of thee
In the first sweet sleep of night,
When the winds are breathing low,
And the stars are shining bright:
I arise from dreams of thee,
And a spirit in my feet
Hath led me—who knows how?
To thy chamber window, Sweet!

The wandering airs they faint
On the dark, the silent stream—
The Champak odours fail
Like sweet thoughts in a dream;
The Nightingale's complaint,
It dies upon her heart;—
As I must on thine,
Oh, belovèd as thou art!

Oh lift me from the grass!
I die! I faint! I fail!
Let thy love in kisses rain
On my lips and eyelids pale.
My cheek is cold and white, alas!
My heart beats loud and fast;—
Oh! press it to thine own again,
Where it will break at last.

I Love Thee
Eliza Acton

I love thee, as I love the calm
    Of sweet, star-lighted hours!
I love thee, as I love the balm
    Of early jes'mine flow'rs.
I love thee, as I love the last
    Rich smile of fading day,
Which lingereth, like the look we cast,
    On rapture pass'd away.
I love thee as I love the tone
    Of some soft-breathing flute
Whose soul is wak'd for me alone,
    When all beside is mute.

I love thee as I love the first
    Young violet of the spring;
Or the pale lily, April-nurs'd,
    To scented blossoming.
I love thee, as I love the full,
    Clear gushings of the song,
Which lonely--sad--and beautiful--
    At night-fall floats along,
Pour'd by the bul-bul forth to greet
    The hours of rest and dew;
When melody and moonlight meet
    To blend their charm, and hue.
I love thee, as the glad bird loves
    The freedom of its wing,

On which delightedly it moves
    In wildest wandering.

I love thee as I love the swell,
    And hush, of some low strain,
Which bringeth, by its gentle spell,
    The past to life again.
Such is the feeling which from thee
    Nought earthly can allure:
'Tis ever link'd to all I see
    Of gifted--high--and pure!

Song: How Sweet I Roam'd from Field to Field
William Blake

How sweet I roam'd from field to field,
    And tasted all the summer's pride,
'Till I the prince of love beheld,
    Who in the sunny beams did glide!

He shew'd me lilies for my hair,
    And blushing roses for my brow;
He led me through his gardens fair,
    Where all his golden pleasures grow.

With sweet May dews my wings were wet,
    And Phoebus fir'd my vocal rage;
He caught me in his silken net,
    And shut me in his golden cage.

He loves to sit and hear me sing,
    Then, laughing, sports and plays with me;
Then stretches out my golden wing,
    And mocks my loss of liberty.

To Jane: The Keen Stars Were Twinkling
Percy Bysshe Shelley

The keen stars were twinkling,
And the fair moon was rising among them,
    Dear Jane!
    The guitar was tinkling,
But the notes were not sweet till you sung them
    Again.

    As the moon's soft splendour
O'er the faint cold starlight of Heaven
    Is thrown,
    So your voice most tender
To the strings without soul had then given
    Its own.

    The stars will awaken,
Though the moon sleep a full hour later,
    Tonight;
    No leaf will be shaken
Whilst the dews of your melody scatter
    Delight.

    Though the sound overpowers,
Sing again, with your dear voice revealing
    A tone
    Of some world far from ours,
Where music and moonlight and feeling
    Are one.

She Walks in Beauty
George Gordon, Lord Byron

She walks in beauty, like the night
  Of cloudless climes and starry skies;
And all that's best of dark and bright
  Meet in her aspect and her eyes;
Thus mellowed to that tender light
  Which heaven to gaudy day denies.

One shade the more, one ray the less,
  Had half impaired the nameless grace
Which waves in every raven tress,
  Or softly lightens o'er her face;
Where thoughts serenely sweet express,
  How pure, how dear their dwelling-place.

And on that cheek, and o'er that brow,
  So soft, so calm, yet eloquent,
The smiles that win, the tints that glow,
  But tell of days in goodness spent,
A mind at peace with all below,
  A heart whose love is innocent!

Delight in Disorder
Robert Herrick

A sweet disorder in the dress
Kindles in clothes a wantonness;
A lawn about the shoulders thrown
Into a fine distraction;
An erring lace, which here and there
Enthrals the crimson stomacher;
A cuff neglectful, and thereby
Ribands to flow confusedly;
A winning wave, deserving note,
In the tempestuous petticoat;
A careless shoe-string, in whose tie
I see a wild civility:
Do more bewitch me, than when art
Is too precise in every part.

My Lady Looks So Gentle and So Pure
Dante Alighieri

My lady looks so gentle and so pure
When yielding salutation by the way,
That the tongue trembles and has naught to say,
And the eyes, which fain would see, may not endure.
And still, amid the praise she hears secure
She walks with humbleness for her array;
Seeming a creature sent from Heaven to stay
On earth, and show a miracle made sure.
She is so pleasant in the eyes of men
That through the sight the inmost heart doth gain
A sweetness which needs proof to know it by:
And from between her lips there seems to move
A soothing essence that is full of love,
Saying for ever to the spirit, "Sigh!"

The Dream
Aphra Behn

All trembling in my arms Aminta lay,
Defending of the bliss I strove to take;
Raising my rapture by her kind delay,
Her force so charming was and weak.
The soft resistance did betray the grant,
While I pressed on the heaven of my desires;
Her rising breasts with nimbler motions pant;
Her dying eyes assume new fires.
Now to the height of languishment she grows,
And still her looks new charms put on;
Now the last mystery of Love she knows,
We sigh, and kiss: I waked, and all was done.

'Twas but a dream, yet by my heart I knew,
Which still was panting, part of it was true:
Oh how I strove the rest to have believed;
Ashamed and angry to be undeceived!

Love
Rupert Brooke

Love is a breach in the walls, a broken gate,
Where that comes in that shall not go again;
Love sells the proud heart's citadel to Fate.
They have known shame, who love unloved. Even then,
When two mouths, thirsty each for each, find slaking,
And agony's forgot, and hushed the crying
Of credulous hearts, in heaven — such are but taking
Their own poor dreams within their arms, and lying
Each in his lonely night, each with a ghost.
Some share that night. But they know love grows colder,
Grows false and dull, that was sweet lies at most.
Astonishment is no more in hand or shoulder,
But darkens, and dies out from kiss to kiss.
All this is love; and all love is but this.

I Love My Love In The Morning
Gerald Griffin

I love my love in the morning,
For she like morn is fair
Her blushing cheek, its crimson streak,
Its clouds her golden hair.

Her glance, its beam, so soft and kind;
Her tears, its dewy showers;
And her voice, the tender whispering wind
That stirs the early bowers.

I love my love in the morning,
I love my love at noon,
For she is bright as the lord of light,
Yet mild as autumn's moon;

Her beauty is my bosom's sun,
Her faith my fostering shade,
And I will love my darling one,
Till even the sun shall fade.

I love my love in the morning,
I love my love at eve;
Her smile's soft play is like the ray
That lights the western heaven;

I loved her when the sun was high,
I loved her when she rose;
But best of all when evening's sigh
Was murmuring at its close.

Now Sleeps the Crimson Petal, Now the White
Alfred, Lord Tennyson

Now sleeps the crimson petal, now the white;
Nor waves the cypress in the palace walk;
Nor winks the gold fin in the porphyry font:
The fire-fly wakens: waken thou with me.

Now droops the milkwhite peacock like a ghost,
And like a ghost she glimmers on to me.

Now lies the Earth all Danaë to the stars,
And all thy heart lies open unto me.

Now slides the silent meteor on, and leaves
A shining furrow, as thy thoughts in me.

Now folds the lily all her sweetness up,
And slips into the bosom of the lake:
So fold thyself, my dearest, thou, and slip
Into my bosom and be lost in me.

Nuptial Sleep
Dante Gabriel Rossetti

At length their long kiss severed, with sweet smart:
And as the last slow sudden drops are shed
From sparkling eaves when all the storm has fled,
So singly flagged the pulses of each heart.
Their bosoms sundered, with the opening start
Of married flowers to either side outspread
From the knit stem; yet still their mouths, burnt red,
Fawned on each other where they lay apart.
Sleep sank them lower than the tide of dreams,
And their dreams watched them sink, and slid away.
Slowly their souls swam up again, through gleams
Of watered light and dull drowned waifs of day;
Till from some wonder of new woods and streams
He woke, and wondered more: for there she lay.

The Sun Rising
John Donne

Busy old fool, unruly Sun,
    Why dost thou thus,
Through windows, and through curtains, call on us?
Must to thy motions lovers' seasons run?
    Saucy pedantic wretch, go chide
    Late school-boys and sour prentices,
  Go tell court-huntsmen that the king will ride,
  Call country ants to harvest offices;
Love, all alike, no season knows nor clime,
Nor hours, days, months, which are the rags of time.

    Thy beams so reverend, and strong
    Why shouldst thou think?
I could eclipse and cloud them with a wink,
But that I would not lose her sight so long.
    If her eyes have not blinded thine,
    Look, and to-morrow late tell me,
  Whether both th' Indias of spice and mine
  Be where thou left'st them, or lie here with me.
Ask for those kings whom thou saw'st yesterday,
And thou shalt hear, "All here in one bed lay."
    She's all states, and all princes I;
    Nothing else is;
Princes do but play us; compared to this,
All honour's mimic, all wealth alchemy.
    Thou, Sun, art half as happy as we,
    In that the world's contracted thus;

Thine age asks ease, and since thy duties be
　To warm the world, that's done in warming us.
Shine here to us, and thou art everywhere;
This bed thy center is, these walls thy sphere.

Extracts from 'Romeo and Juliet'
William Shakespeare

Love is a smoke made with the fume of sighs;
Being purg'd, a fire sparkling in lovers' eyes;
Being vex'd, a sea norish'd with lovers' tears;
What is it else? A madness most discreet,
A choking gall, and a preserving sweet.
(Act l.i)

O, she doth teach the torches to burn bright!
Her beauty hangs upon the cheek of night
Like a rich jewel in an Ethiop's ear;
Beauty too rich for use, for earth too dear!
So shows a snowy dove trooping with crow,
As yonder lady o'er her fellows shows.
The measure done, I'll watch her place of stand,
And, touching hers, make blessed my rude hand.
Did my heart love till now? Forswear it, sight!
For I ne'er saw true beauty till this night.
(Act l.v)

But soft! What light through yonder window breaks?
It is the East and Juliet is the sun!
Arise, fair sun, and kill the envious moon,
Who is already sick and pale with grief
That thou her maid art more fair than she.
Be not her maid, since she is envious.
Her vestal livery is but sick and green,
And none but fools do wear it. Cast it off.

It is my lady; O it is my love!
O that she knew she were!
She speaks, yet she says nothing. What of that?
Her eye discourses; I will answer it.
I am too bold; 'tis not to me she speaks.
Two of the fairest stars in all the heaven,
Having some business, do entreat her eyes
To twinkle in their spheres till they return.
What if he eyes were there, they in her head?
The brightness of her cheek would shame those stars
As daylight doth a lamp; her eyes in heaven
Would through the airy region stream so bright
That birds would sing and think it were not night.
See how she leans her cheek upon her hand!
O that I were a glove upon that hand,
That I might torch that cheek!
(Act ll.ii)

MARRIAGE

To My Dear and Loving Husband
Anne Bradstreet

If ever two were one, then surely we.
If ever man were loved by wife, then thee;
If ever wife was happy in a man,
Compare with me ye women if you can.
I prize thy love more than whole mines of gold,
Or all the riches that the East doth hold.
My love is such that rivers cannot quench,
Nor ought but love from thee give recompense.
Thy love is such I can no way repay;
The heavens reward thee manifold, I pray.
Then while we live, in love let's so persever,
That when we live no more we may live ever.

At the Wedding March
Gerard Manley Hopkins

God with honour hang your head,
Groom, and grace you, bride, your bed
With lissome scions, sweet scions,
Out of hallowed bodies bred.

Each be other's comfort kind:
Déep, déeper than divined,
Divine charity, dear charity,
Fast you ever, fast bind.

Then let the March tread our ears:
I to him turn with tears
Who to wedlock, his wonder wedlock,
Déals tríumph and immortal years.

The Bridal Veil
Alice Cary

We're married, they say, and you think you have won me,--
Well, take this white veil from my head, and look on me;
Here's matter to vex you, and matter to grieve you,
Here's doubt to distrust you, and faith to believe you,--
I am all as you see, common earth, common dew;
Be wary, and mould me to roses, not rue!

Ah! shake out the filmy thing, fold after fold,
And see if you have me to keep and to hold,--
Look close on my heart--see the worst of its sinning,--
It is not yours to-day for the yesterday's winning--
The past is not mine--I am too proud to borrow--
You must grow to new heights if I love you to-morrow.

I have wings flattened down and hid under my veil:
They are subtle as light--you can never undo them,
And swift in their flight--you can never pursue them,
And spite of all clasping, and spite of all bands,
I can slip like a shadow, a dream, from your hands.

Nay, call me not cruel, and fear not to take me,
I am yours for my life-time, to be what you make me,--
To wear my white veil for a sign, or a cover,
As you shall be proven my lord, or my lover;
A cover for peace that is dead, or a token
Of bliss that can never be written or spoken.

Wedlock
Benjamin Franklin

Wedlock, as old men note, hath likened been,
Unto a public crowd or common rout;
Where those that are without would fain get in,
And those that are within, would fain get out.
Grief often treads upon the heels of pleasure,
Marry'd in haste, we oft repent at leisure;
Some by experience find these words missplaced,
Marry'd at leisure, they repent in haste.

Marriage

Bridal Song
George Chapman

O come, soft rest of cares! come, Night!
    Come, naked Virtue's only tire,
The reapèd harvest of the light
   Bound up in sheaves of sacred fire,
    Love calls to war:
       Sighs his alarms,
    Lips his swords are,
       The fields his arms.

Come, Night, and lay thy velvet hand
   On glorious Day's outfacing face;
And all thy crownèd flames command
   For torches to our nuptial grace.
    Love calls to war:
       Sighs his alarms,
    Lips his swords are,
       The field his arms.

To the Virgins, to Make Much of Time
Robert Herrick

Gather ye rosebuds while ye may,
   Old Time is still a-flying;
And this same flower that smiles today
   Tomorrow will be dying.

The glorious lamp of heaven, the sun,
   The higher he's a-getting,
The sooner will his race be run,
   And nearer he's to setting.

That age is best which is the first,
   When youth and blood are warmer;
But being spent, the worse, and worst
   Times still succeed the former.

Then be not coy, but use your time,
   And while ye may, go marry;
For having lost but once your prime,
   You may forever tarry.

Sonnet VIII
William Shakespeare

Music to hear, why hear'st thou music sadly?
Sweets with sweets war not, joy delights in joy:
Why lov'st thou that which thou receiv'st not gladly,
Or else receiv'st with pleasure thine annoy?
If the true concord of well-tuned sounds,
By unions married, do offend thine ear,
They do but sweetly chide thee, who confounds
In singleness the parts that thou shouldst bear.
Mark how one string, sweet husband to another,
Strikes each in each by mutual ordering;
Resembling sire and child and happy mother,
Who, all in one, one pleasing note do sing:
   Whose speechless song being many, seeming one,
   Sings this to thee: 'Thou single wilt prove none.'

The Prophet, on Marriage
Khalil Gibran

You were born together, and together you shall be
forevermore.
You shall be together when the white wings of death scatter
your days.
Ay, you shall be together even in the silent memory of God.
But let there be spaces in your togetherness,
And let the winds of the heavens dance between you.

Love one another, but make not a bond of love:
Let it rather be a moving sea between the shores of your
souls.
Fill each other's cup but drink not from one cup.
Give one another of your bread but eat not from the same
loaf
Sing and dance together and be joyous, but let each one of
you be alone,
Even as the strings of a lute are alone though they quiver
with the same music.

Give your hearts, but not into each other's keeping.
For only the hand of Life can contain your hearts.
And stand together yet not too near together:
For the pillars of the temple stand apart,
And the oak tree and the cypress grow not in each other's
shadow.

To Silvia, To Wed
Robert Herrick

Let us, though late, at last, my Silvia, wed;
And loving lie in one devoted bed.
Thy watch may stand, my minutes fly post haste;
No sound calls back the year that once is past.
Then, sweetest Silvia, let's no longer stay;
True love, we know, precipitates delay.
Away with doubts, all scruples hence remove!
No man, at one time, can be wise, and love.

The Good-Morrow
John Donne

I wonder, by my troth, what thou and I
Did, till we loved? Were we not weaned till then?
But sucked on country pleasures, childishly?
Or snorted we in the Seven Sleepers' den?
'Twas so; but this, all pleasures fancies be.
If ever any beauty I did see,
Which I desired, and got, 'twas but a dream of thee.

And now good-morrow to our waking souls,
Which watch not one another out of fear;
For love, all love of other sights controls,
And makes one little room an everywhere.
Let sea-discoverers to new worlds have gone,
Let maps to other, worlds on worlds have shown,
Let us possess one world, each hath one, and is one.

My face in thine eye, thine in mine appears,
And true plain hearts do in the faces rest;
Where can we find two better hemispheres,
Without sharp north, without declining west?
Whatever dies, was not mixed equally;
If our two loves be one, or, thou and I
Love so alike, that none do slacken, none can die.

Love is Enough
William Morris

Love is enough: though the World be a-waning,
And the woods have no voice but the voice of complaining,
  Though the sky be too dark for dim eyes to discover
The gold-cups and daisies fair blooming thereunder,
Though the hills be held shadows, and the sea a dark
wonder,
  And this day draw a veil over all deeds pass'd over,
Yet their hands shall not tremble, their feet shall not falter;
The void shall not weary, the fear shall not alter
  These lips and these eyes of the loved and the lover.

I Gave Myself To Him
Emily Dickinson

I gave myself to him,
And took himself for pay.
The solemn contract of a life
Was ratified this way.

The wealth might disappoint,
Myself a poorer prove
Than this great purchaser suspect,
The daily own of Love

Depreciate the vision;
But, till the merchant buy,
Still fable, in the isles of spice,
The subtle cargoes lie.

At least, 't is mutual risk,—
Some found it mutual gain;
Sweet debt of Life,—each night to owe,
Insolvent, every noon.

The Wedding Night
Johann Wolfgang von Goethe

Within the chamber, far away
From the glad feast, sits Love in dread
Lest guests disturb, in wanton play,
The silence of the bridal bed.
His torch's pale flame serves to gild
The scene with mystic sacred glow;
The room with incense-clouds is fil'd,
That ye may perfect rapture know.
How beats thy heart, when thou dost hear
The chime that warns thy guests to fly!
How glow'st thou for those lips so dear,
That soon are mute, and nought deny!
With her into the holy place
Thou hast'nest then, to perfect all;
The fire the warder's hands embrace,
Grows, like a night-light, dim and small.
How heaves her bosom, and how burns
Her face at every fervent kiss!
Her coldness now to trembling turns,
Thy daring now a duty is.
Love helps thee to undress her fast,
But thou art twice as fast as he;
And then he shuts both eye at last,
With sly and roguish modesty.

My Wife
Robert Louis Stevenson

Trusty, dusky, vivid, true,
With eyes of gold and bramble-dew,
Steel-true and blade-straight,
The great artificer
Made my mate.

Honour, anger, valour, fire;
A love that life could never tire,
Death quench or evil stir,
The mighty master
Gave to her.

Teacher, tender, comrade, wife,
A fellow-farer true through life,
Heart-whole and soul-free
The august father
Gave to me.

Sonnet III
William Shakespeare

Look in thy glass and tell the face thou viewest
Now is the time that face should form another;
Whose fresh repair if now thou not renewest,
Thou dost beguile the world, unbless some mother.
For where is she so fair whose uneared womb
Disdains the tillage of thy husbandry?
Or who is he so fond will be the tomb
Of his self-love, to stop posterity?
Thou art thy mother's glass and she in thee
Calls back the lovely April of her prime;
So thou through windows of thine age shalt see,
Despite of wrinkles, this thy golden time.
　　But if thou live, remembered not to be,
　　Die single and thine image dies with thee.

Words on Feeling Safe
George Eliot

Oh the comfort of feeling safe
with a person;
having neither to weigh thoughts,
nor measure words,
but to pour them all out
just as chaff and grain together,
knowing that a faithful hand
will take and sift them,
keeping what is worth keeping
and with a breath of kindness,
blow the rest away.

Satires of Circumstances, I. At Tea
Thomas Hardy

The kettle descants in a cosy drone,
And the young wife looks in her husband's face,
And then in her guest's, and shows in her own
Her sense that she fills an envied place;
And the visiting lady is all abloom,
And says there was never so sweet a room.
And the happy young housewife does not know
That the woman beside her was his first choice,
Till the fates ordained it could not be so....
Betraying nothing in look or voice
The guest sits smiling and sips her tea,
And he throws her a stray glance yearningly.

Marriage Morning
Alfred, Lord Tennyson

Light, so low upon earth,
 You send a flash to the sun.
Here is the golden close of love,
 All my wooing is done.
Oh, all the woods and the meadows,
 Woods, where we hid from the wet,
Stiles where we stayed to be kind,
 Meadows in which we met!
Light, so low in the vale
 You flash and lighten afar,
For this is the golden morning of love,
 And you are his morning star.
Flash, I am coming, I come,
 By meadow and stile and wood,
Oh, lighten into my eyes and my heart,
 Into my heart and my blood!
Heart, are you great enough
 For a love that never tires?
O heart, are you great enough for love?
 I have heard of thorns and briers.
Over the thorns and briers,
 Over the meadows and stiles,
Over the world to the end of it
 Flash of a million miles.

An Epitaph Upon Husband and Wife
Who died and were buried together
Richard Crashaw

To these whom death again did wed
This grave 's the second marriage-bed.
For though the hand of Fate could force
'Twixt soul and body a divorce,
It could not sever man and wife,
Because they both lived but one life.
Peace, good reader, do not weep;
Peace, the lovers are asleep.
They, sweet turtles, folded lie
In the last knot that love could tie.
Let them sleep, let them sleep on,
Till the stormy night be gone,
And the eternal morrow dawn;
Then the curtains will be drawn,
And they wake into a light
Whose day shall never die in night.

Remember
Christina Rossetti

Remember me when I am gone away,
    Gone far away into the silent land;
    When you can no more hold me by the hand,
Nor I half turn to go yet turning stay.
Remember me when no more day by day
    You tell me of our future that you plann'd:
    Only remember me; you understand
It will be late to counsel then or pray.
Yet if you should forget me for a while
    And afterwards remember, do not grieve:
    For if the darkness and corruption leave
    A vestige of the thoughts that once I had,
Better by far you should forget and smile
    Than that you should remember and be sad.

The Passionate Shepherd to His Love
Christopher Marlowe

Come live with me and be my love,
And we will all the pleasures prove,
That Valleys, groves, hills, and fields,
Woods, or steepy mountain yields.

And we will sit upon the Rocks,
Seeing the Shepherds feed their flocks,
By shallow Rivers to whose falls
Melodious birds sing Madrigals.

And I will make thee beds of Roses
And a thousand fragrant posies,
A cap of flowers, and a kirtle
Embroidered all with leaves of Myrtle;

A gown made of the finest wool
Which from our pretty Lambs we pull;
Fair lined slippers for the cold,
With buckles of the purest gold;

A belt of straw and Ivy buds,
With Coral clasps and Amber studs:
And if these pleasures may thee move,
Come live with me, and be my love.

The Shepherds' Swains shall dance and sing
For thy delight each May-morning:
If these delights thy mind may move,
Then live with me, and be my love.

The Nymph's Reply to the Shepherd
Sir Walter Raleigh

If all the world and love were young,
And truth in every Shepherd's tongue,
These pretty pleasures might me move,
To live with thee, and be thy love.

Time drives the flocks from field to fold,
When Rivers rage and Rocks grow cold,
And Philomel becometh dumb,
The rest complains of cares to come.

The flowers do fade, and wanton fields,
To wayward winter reckoning yields,
A honey tongue, a heart of gall,
Is fancy's spring, but sorrow's fall.

Thy gowns, thy shoes, thy beds of Roses,
Thy cap, thy kirtle, and thy posies
Soon break, soon wither, soon forgotten:
In folly ripe, in reason rotten.

Thy belt of straw and Ivy buds,
The Coral clasps and amber studs,
All these in me no means can move
To come to thee and be thy love.

But could youth last, and love still breed,
Had joys no date, nor age no need,
Then these delights my mind might move
To live with thee, and be thy love.

A Marriage Ring
George Crabbe

The ring, so worn as you behold,
So thin, so pale, is yet of gold:
The passion such it was to prove—
Worn with life's care, love yet was love.

A Letter To Daphis
Anne Finch, Countess of Winchelsea

This to the crown and blessing of my life,
The much loved husband of a happy wife;
To him whose constant passion found the art
To win a stubborn and ungrateful heart,
And to the world by tenderest proof discovers
They err, who say that husbands can't be lovers.
With such return of passion as is due,
Daphnis I love, Daphnis my thoughts pursue;
Daphnis my hopes and joys are bounded all in you.
Even I, for Daphnis' and my promise' sake,
What I in women censure, undertake.
But this from love, not vanity, proceeds;
You know who writes, and I who 'tis that reads.
Judge not my passion by my want of skill:
Many love well, though they express it ill;
And I your censure could with pleasure bear,
Would you but soon return, and speak it here.

Nuptial Sleep
Dante Gabriel Rossetti

At length their long kiss severed, with sweet smart:
And as the last slow sudden drops are shed
From sparkling eaves when all the storm has fled,
So singly flagged the pulses of each heart.
Their bosoms sundered, with the opening start
Of married flowers to either side outspread
From the knit stem; yet still their mouths, burnt red,
Fawned on each other where they lay apart.
Sleep sank them lower than the tide of dreams,
And their dreams watched them sink, and slid away.
Slowly their souls swam up again, through gleams
Of watered light and dull drowned waifs of day;
Till from some wonder of new woods and streams
He woke, and wondered more: for there she lay.

Before the Birth of One of Her Children
Anne Bradstreet

All things within this fading world hath end,
Adversity doth still our joyes attend;
No ties so strong, no friends so dear and sweet,
But with death's parting blow is sure to meet.
The sentence past is most irrevocable,
A common thing, yet oh inevitable.
How soon, my Dear, death may my steps attend,
How soon't may be thy Lot to lose thy friend,
We are both ignorant, yet love bids me
These farewell lines to recommend to thee,
That when that knot's untied that made us one,
I may seem thine, who in effect am none.
And if I see not half my dayes that's due,
What nature would, God grant to yours and you;
The many faults that well you know I have
Let be interr'd in my oblivious grave;
If any worth or virtue were in me,
Let that live freshly in thy memory
And when thou feel'st no grief, as I no harms,
Yet love thy dead, who long lay in thine arms.
And when thy loss shall be repaid with gains
Look to my little babes, my dear remains.
And if thou love thyself, or loved'st me,
These o protect from step Dames injury.
And if chance to thine eyes shall bring this verse,
With some sad sighs honour my absent Herse;
And kiss this paper for thy loves dear sake,
Who with salt tears this last Farewel did take.

Marriage
Mary Weston Fordham

The die is cast, come weal, come woe,
Two lives are joined together,
For better or for worse, the link
Which naught but death can sever.
The die is cast, come grief, come joy,
Come richer, or come poorer,
If love but binds the mystic tie,
Blest is the bridal hour.

To One Persuading A Lady to Marriage
Katherine Philips ('Orinda')

Forbear, bold youth; all 's heaven here,
  And what you do aver
To others courtship may appear,
  'Tis sacrilege to her.
She is a public deity;
  And were 't not very odd
She should dispose herself to be
  A petty household god?

First make the sun in private shine
  And bid the world adieu,
That so he may his beams confine
  In compliment to you:
But if of that you do despair,
  Think how you did amiss
To strive to fix her beams which are
  More bright and large than his.

A Letter To Her Husband, Absent Upon Publick Employment
Anne Bradstreet

My head, my heart, mine Eyes, my life, nay more,
My joy, my Magazine of earthly store,
If two be one, as surely thou and I,
How stayest thou there, whilst I at Ipswich lye?
So many steps, head from the heart to sever
If but a neck, soon should we be together:
I like the earth this season, mourn in black,
My Sun is gone so far in's Zodiack,
Whom whilst I 'joy'd, nor storms, nor frosts I felt,
His warmth such frigid colds did cause to melt.
My chilled limbs now nummed lye forlorn;
Return, return sweet Sol from Capricorn;
In this dead time, alas, what can I more
Then view those fruits which through thy heat I bore?
Which sweet contentment yield me for a space,
True living Pictures of their Fathers face.
O strange effect! now thou art Southward gone,
I weary grow, the tedious day so long;
But when thou Northward to me shalt return,
I wish my Sun may never set, but burn
Within the Cancer of my glowing breast,
The welcome house of him my dearest guest.
Where ever, ever stay, and go not thence,
Till natures sad decree shall call thee hence;
Flesh of thy flesh, bone of thy bone,
I here, thou there, yet both but one.

Bridal Song
John Fletcher

Cynthia, to thy power and thee
    We obey.
Joy to this great company!
    And no day
Come to steal this night away
  Till the rites of love are ended,
And the lusty bridegroom say,
  Welcome, light, of all befriended!

Pace out, you watery powers below;
    Let your feet,   10
Like the galleys when they row,
    Even beat;
Let your unknown measures, set
  To the still winds, tell to all
That gods are come, immortal, great,
  To honour this great nuptial!

Bridal Song
William Shakespeare

Roses, their sharp spines being gone,
Not royal in their smells alone,
  But in their hue;
Maiden pinks, of odour faint,
Daisies smell-less, yet most quaint,
  And sweet thyme true;

Primrose, firstborn child of Ver;
Merry springtime's harbinger,
  With her bells dim;
Oxlips in their cradles growing,
Marigolds on death-beds blowing,
  Larks'-heels trim;

All dear Nature's children sweet
Lie 'fore bride and bridegroom's feet,
  Blessing their sense!
Not an angel of the air,
Bird melodious or bird fair,
  Be absent hence!

The crow, the slanderous cuckoo, nor
The boding raven, nor chough hoar,
  Nor chattering pye,
May on our bride-house perch or sing,
Or with them any discord bring,
  But from it fly!

The Happy Husband
Samuel Taylor Coleridge

Oft, oft, methinks, the while with thee
I breathe, as from the heart, thy dear
And dedicated bame, I hear
A promise and a mystery,
A pledge of more than passing life,
Yea, in that very name of wife!

A pulse of love that ne'er can sleep!
A feeling that upbraids the heart
With happiness beyond desert,
That gladness half requests to weep!
Nor bless I not the keener sense
And unalarming turbulence.

Of transient joys, that ask no sting
From jealous fears, or coy denying;
But born beneath Love's brooding wing,
And into tenderness soon dying.
Wheel out their giddy moment, then
Resign the soul to love again;

A more precipitated vein
Of notes that eddy in the flow
Of smoothest song, they come, they go,
And leave their sweeter understrain
Its own sweet self-a love of thee
That seems, yet cannot greater be!

Ruth
Thomas Hood

She stood breast high amid the corn,
Clasped by the golden light of morn,
Like the sweetheart of the sun,
Who many a glowing kiss had won.

On her cheek an autumn flush,
Deeply ripened;—such a blush
In the midst of brown was born,
Like red poppies grown with corn.

Round her eyes her tresses fell,
Which were blackest none could tell,
But long lashes veiled a light,
That had else been all too bright.

And her hat, with shady brim,
Made her tressy forehead dim;—
Thus she stood amid the stooks,
Praising God with sweetest looks:—

Sure, I said, heaven did not mean,
Where I reap thou shouldst but glean,
Lay thy sheaf adown and come,
Share my harvest and my home.

The Angel in the House (excerpt)
Coventry Patmore

THE DEAN'S CONSENT

The ladies rose. I held the door,
  And sigh'd, as her departing grace
Assur'd me that she always wore
  And heart as happy as her face;
And, jealous of the winds that blew,
  I dreaded, o'er the tasteless wine,
What fortune momently might do
  To hurt the hope that she 'd be mine.

Towards my mark the Dean's talk set:
  He praised my "Notes on Abury,"
Read when the Association met
  At Sarum; he was pleas'd to see
I had not stopp'd, as some men had,
  At Wrangler and Prize Poet; last,
He hop'd the business was not bad
  I came about: then the wine pass'd.

A full glass prefaced my reply:
  I lov'd his daughter, Honor; I told
My estate and prospects; might I try
  To win her? At my words so bold
My sick heart sank. Then he: He gave
  His glad consent, if I could get
Her love. A dear, good Girl! she 'd have

Only three thousand pounds as yet;
More by and by. Yes, his good will
  Should go with me; he would not stir;

He and my father in old time still
  Wish'd I should one day marry her;
But God so seldom lets us take
  Our chosen pathway, when it lies
In steps that either mar or make
  Or alter others' destinies,
That, though his blessing and his pray'r
  Had help'd, should help, my suit, yet he
Left all to me, his passive share
  Consent and opportunity.

My chance, he hop'd, was good: I'd won
  Some name already; friends and place
Appear'd within my reach, but none
  Her mind and manners would not grace.
Girls love to see the men in whom
  They invest their vanities admir'd;
Besides, where goodness is, there room
  For good to work will be desir'd.
'T was so with one now pass'd away;
  And what she was at twenty-two,
Honor was now; and he might say
  Mine was a choice I could not rue.

He ceas'd, and gave his hand. He had won
  (And all my heart was in my word)
From me the affection of a son,

Whichever fortune Heaven conferr'd!
Well, well, would I take more wine? Then go
  To her; she makes tea on the lawn
These fine warm afternoons. And so
  We went whither my soul was drawn;
And her light-hearted ignorance
  Of interest in our discourse
Fill'd me with love, and seem'd to enhance
  Her beauty with pathetic force,
As, through the flowery mazes sweet,
  Fronting the wind that flutter'd blithe,
And lov'd her shape, and kiss'd her feet,
  Shown to their insteps proud and lithe,
She approach'd, all mildness and young trust,
  And ever her chaste and noble air
Gave to love's feast its choicest gust,
  A vague, faint augury of despair.

HONORIA'S SURRENDER

From little signs, like little stars,
  Whose faint impression on the sense
The very looking straight at mars,
  Or only seen by confluence;
From instinct of a mutual thought,
  Whence sanctity of manners flow'd;
From chance unconscious, and from what
  Concealment, overconscious, show'd;
Her hand's less weight upon my arm,
  Her lovelier mien; that match'd with this;

Marriage

I found, and felt with strange alarm,
  I stood committed to my bliss.

I grew assur'd, before I ask'd,
  That she 'd be mine without reserve,
And in her unclaim'd graces bask'd,
  At leisure, till the time should serve,
With just enough of dread to thrill
  The hope, and make it trebly dear;
Thus loth to speak the word to kill
  Either the hope or happy fear.

Till once, through lanes returning late,
  Her laughing sisters lagg'd behind;
And, ere we reach'd her father's gate,
  We paus'd with one presentient mind;
And, in the dim and perfum'd mist,
  Their coming stay'd, who, friends to me,
And very women, lov'd to assist
  Love's timid opportunity.

Twice rose, twice died my trembling word;
  The faint and frail Cathedral chimes
Spake time in music, and we heard
  The chafers rustling in the limes.
Her dress, that touch'd me where I stood,
  The warmth of her confided arm,
Her bosom's gentle neighborhood,
  Her pleasure in her power to charm;
Her look, her love, her form, her touch,
  The least seem'd most by blissful turn,

Blissful but that it pleas'd too much,
  And taught the wayward soul to yearn.
It was as if a harp with wires
  Was travers'd by the breath I drew;
And, oh, sweet meeting of desires,
  She, answering, own'd that she lov'd too.

Honoria was to be my bride!
  The hopeless heights of hope were scal'd;
The summit won, I paus'd and sigh'd,
  As if success itself had fail'd.
It seem'd as if my lips approach'd
  To touch at Tantalus' reward,
And rashly on Eden life encroach'd,
  Half-blinded by the flaming sword.
The whole world's wealthiest and its best,
  So fiercely sought, appear'd, when found,
Poor in its need to be possess'd,
  Poor from its very want of bound.

My queen was crouching at my side,
  By love unsceptred and brought low,
Her awful garb of maiden pride
  All melted into tears like snow;
The mistress of my reverent thought,
  Whose praise was all I ask'd of fame,
In my close-watch'd approval sought
  Protection as from danger and blame;
Her soul, which late I lov'd to invest
  With pity for my poor desert,

Buried its face within my breast,
  Like a pet fawn by hunters hurt.

THE MARRIED LOVER

Why, having won her, do I woo?
  Because her spirit's vestal grace
Provokes me always to pursue,
  But, spirit-like, eludes embrace;
Because her womanhood is such
  That, as on court-days subjects kiss
The Queen's hand, yet so near a touch
  Affirms no mean familiarness,
Nay, rather marks more fair the height
  Which can with safety so neglect
To dread, as lower ladies might,
  That grace could meet with disrespect,
Thus she with happy favor feeds
  Allegiance from a love so high
That thence no false conceit proceeds
  Of difference bridged, or state put by;
Because, although in act and word
  As lowly as a wife can be,
Her manners, when they call me lord,
  Remind me 't is by courtesy;
Not with her least consent of will,
  Which would my proud affection hurt,
But by the noble style that still
  Imputes an unattain'd desert;
Because her gay and lofty brows,
  When all is won which hope can ask,

Reflect a light of hopeless snows
   That bright in virgin ether bask;
Because, though free of the outer court

   I am, this Temple keeps its shrine
Sacred to Heaven; because, in short,
   She's not and never can be mine.

Feasts satiate; stars distress with height;
   Friendship means well, but misses reach,
And wearies in its best delight
   Vex'd with the vanities of speech;
Too long regarded, roses even
   Afflict the mind with fond unrest;
And to converse direct with Heaven
   Is oft a labor in the breast;
Whate'er the up-looking soul admires,
   Whate'er the senses' banquet be,
Fatigues at last with vain desires,
   Or sickens by satiety;
But truly my delight was more
   In her to whom I'm bound for aye
Yesterday than the day before,
   And more to-day than yesterday.

Satires of Circumstance IX. At the Altar-Rail
Thomas Hardy

"My bride is not coming, alas!" says the groom,
And the telegram shakes in his hand. "I own
It was hurried! We met at a dancing-room
When I went to the Cattle-Show alone,
And then, next night, where the Fountain leaps,
And the Street of the Quarter-Circle sweeps.

"Ay, she won me to ask her to be my wife -
'Twas foolish perhaps! to forsake the ways
Of the flaring town for a farmer's life.
She agreed. And we fixed it. Now she says:
'It's sweet of you, dear, to prepare me a nest,
But a swift, short, gay life suits me best.
What I really am you have never gleaned;
I had eaten the apple ere you were weaned.'"

A Chinese Wedding Poem
Anonymous

I want to be your friend
For ever and ever without break or decay.
When the hills are all flat
And the rivers are all dry,
When it lightens and thunders in winter,
When it rains and snows in summer,
When Heaven and Earth mingle
Not 'til then will I part from you.

Sonnet CXVI
William Shakespeare

Let me not to the marriage of true minds
Admit impediments. Love is not love
Which alters when it alteration finds,
Or bends with the remover to remove:
O no; it is an ever-fixed mark,
That looks on tempests, and is never shaken;
It is the star to every wandering bark,
Whose worth's unknown, although his height be taken.
Love's not Time's fool, though rosy lips and cheeks
Within his bending sickle's compass come;
Love alters not with his brief hours and weeks,
But bears it out even to the edge of doom.
If this be error and upon me proved,
I never writ, nor no man ever loved.

Extract from *Love Lives*
John Clare

Love lives beyond
The tomb, the earth, which fades like dew,
I love the fond,
The faithful, and the true.
Love lies in sleep,
The happiness of healthy dreams,
Eve's dews may weep,
But love delightful seems.
'Tis seen in flowers,
And in the even's pearly dew
On earth's green hours,
And in the heaven's eternal blue.

'Tis heard in spring
When light and sunbeams, warm and kind,
On angel's wing
Bring love and music to the wind.
And where is voice
So young, so beautiful, so sweet
As nature's choice,
Where spring and lovers meet?
Love lies beyond
The tomb, the earth, the flowers, and dew.
I love the fond,
The faithful, young, and true.

Extract from *Arcadia*
Sir Philip Sidney

My true-love hath my heart and I have his,
By just exchange one for the other given:
I hold his dear, and mine he cannot miss;
There never was a bargain better driven.
His heart in me keeps me and him in one;
My heart in him, his thoughts and senses guides:
He loves my heart, for once it was his own;
I cherish his because in me it bides.
His heart his wound received from my sight;
My heart was wounded with his wounded heart;
For as from me on him his hurt did light,
So still, methought, in me his hurt did smart:
Both equal hurt, in this change sought our bliss,
My true love hath my heart and I have his.

Extract from *The Anniversary*
John Donne

All kings, and all their favourites,
All glory of honours, beauties, wits,
The sun itself, which makes times, as they pass,
Is elder by a year now than it was
When thou and I first one another saw:
All other things to their destruction draw,
Only our love hath no decay;
This no tomorrow hath, nor yesterday,
Running it never runs from us away,
But truly keeps his first, last, everlasting day.

HAPPILY EVERY AFTER

Jenny Kiss'd Me
Leigh Hunt

Jenny kiss'd me when we met,
   Jumping from the chair she sat in;
Time, you thief, who love to get
   Sweets into your list, put that in!
Say I'm weary, say I'm sad,
   Say that health and wealth have miss'd me,
Say I'm growing old, but add,
   Jenny kiss'd me.

Bright Star
John Keats

Bright star, would I were stedfast as thou art—
    Not in lone splendour hung aloft the night
And watching, with eternal lids apart,
    Like nature's patient, sleepless Eremite,
The moving waters at their priestlike task
    Of pure ablution round earth's human shores,
Or gazing on the new soft-fallen mask
    Of snow upon the mountains and the moors—
No—yet still stedfast, still unchangeable,
    Pillow'd upon my fair love's ripening breast,
To feel for ever its soft fall and swell,
    Awake for ever in a sweet unrest,
Still, still to hear her tender-taken breath,
And so live ever—or else swoon to death.

She Comes Not When Noon is On the Roses
Herbert Trench

She comes not when Noon is on the roses—
    Too bright is Day.
She comes not to the Soul till it reposes
    From work and play.

But when Night is on the hills, and the great Voices
    Roll in from Sea,
By starlight and by candlelight and dreamlight
    She comes to me.

At Last
Elizabeth Akers Allen

At last, when all the summer shine
    That warmed life's early hours is past,
Your loving fingers seek for mine
    And hold them close—at last—at last!
Not oft the robin comes to build
    Its nest upon the leafless bough
By autumn robbed, by winter chilled,—
    But you, dear heart, you love me now.

Though there are shadows on my brow
    And furrows on my cheek, in truth,—
The marks where Time's remorseless plough
    Broke up the blooming sward of Youth,—
Though fled is every girlish grace
    Might win or hold a lover's vow,
Despite my sad and faded face,
    And darkened heart, you love me now!

I count no more my wasted tears;
    They left no echo of their fall;
I mourn no more my lonesome years;
    This blessed hour atones for all.
I fear not all that Time or Fate
    May bring to burden heart or brow,—
Strong in the love that came so late,
    Our souls shall keep it always now!

Amoretti, Sonnet #75
Edmund Spenser

One day I wrote her name upon the strand,
>But came the waves and washed it away:
>Again I write it with a second hand,
>But came the tide, and made my pains his prey.
Vain man, said she, that doest in vain assay,
>A mortal thing so to immortalize,
>For I myself shall like to this decay,
>And eek my name be wiped out likewise.
Not so, (quod I) let baser things devise
>To die in dust, but you shall live by fame:
>My verse, your virtues rare shall eternize,
>And in the heavens write your glorious name.
Where whenas death shall all the world subdue,
>Our love shall live, and later life renew.

Freedom and Love
Thomas Campbell

How delicious is the winning
Of a kiss at Love's beginning,
When two mutual hearts are sighing
For the knot there's no untying!

Yet remember, 'midst your wooing,
Love has bliss, but Love has ruing;
Other smiles may make you fickle,
Tears for other charms may trickle.

Love he comes, and Love he tarries,
Just as fate or fancy carries;
Longest stays when sorest chidden,
Laughs and flies when press'd and bidden.

Bind the sea to slumber stilly,
Bind its odour to the lily,
Bind the aspen ne'er to quiver,
Then bind Love to last for ever.

Love's a fire that needs renewal
Of fresh beauty for its fuel;
Love's wing moults when caged and captured,
Only free he soars enraptured.

Can you keep the bee from ranging,
Or the ringdove's neck from changing?
No! nor fetter'd Love from dying
In the knot there's no untying.

If Thou Must Love Me
Elizabeth Barrett Browning

If thou must love me, let it be for nought
Except for love's sake only. Do not say,
"I love her for her smile—her look—her way
Of speaking gently,—for a trick of thought
That falls in well with mine, and certes brought
A sense of pleasant ease on such a day"—
For these things in themselves, Belovèd, may
Be changed, or change for thee—and love, so wrought,
May be unwrought so. Neither love me for
Thine own dear pity's wiping my cheeks dry:
A creature might forget to weep, who bore
Thy comfort long, and lose thy love thereby!
But love me for love's sake, that evermore
Thou mayst love on, through love's eternity.

When You Are Old
W.B. Yeats

When you are old and grey and full of sleep,
And nodding by the fire, take down this book,
And slowly read, and dream of the soft look
Your eyes had once and of their shadows deep;

How many loved your moments of glad grace,
And loved your beauty with love false or true;
But one man loved the pilgrim soul in you,
And loved the sorrows of your changing face.

And bending down beside the glowing bars
Murmur, a little sadly, how love fled
And paced upon the mountains overhead
And hid his face amid a crowd of stars.

An Evening Song
Sidney Lanier

Look off, dear Love, across the shallow sands,
And mark yon meeting of the sun and the sea,
How long they kiss in sight of all the lands.
Ah! longer, longer we.
Now in the sea's red vintage melts the sun,
As Egypt's red pearl dissolved in rosy wine,
And Cleopatra night drinks all. 'Tis done,
Love, lay thine hand in mine.
Come forth, sweet stars, and comfort heaven's heart;
Glimmer, ye waves, round else unlighted sands.
O night! divorce our sun and sky apart
Never our lips, our hands.

My Grandmother's Love Letters
Hart Crane

There are no stars tonight
But those of memory.
Yet how much room for memory there is
In the loose girdle of soft rain.

There is even room enough
For the letters of my mother's mother,
Elizabeth,
That have been pressed so long Into a corner of the roof
That they are brown and soft,
And liable to melt as snow.
Over the greatness of such space
Steps must be gentle.
It is all hung by an invisible white hair.
It tremble as birch limbs webbing the air.

And I ask myself:

"Are your fingers long enough to play
Old keys that are but echoes:
Is the silence strong enough
To carry back the music to its source
And back to you again
As though to her?"

Yet I would lead my grandmother by the hand
Through much of what she would not understand;
And so I stumble. And the rain continues on the roof
With such a sound of gently pitying laughter.

A Dog Who's Lost
Richard Happer

Like rhubarb without custard
Or ham what's got no mustard
Like a skylark without wings
And a playpark with no swings

A door without a latch
Socks that do not match
Fingers without thumbs
Or sticks what's lost their drums

Like Bond with no Martini
Or a king without his queenie
Like Tom apart from Jerry
A Christmas that's not merry

A singer with no song
A ding without a dong
Lemon minus lime
A poem with no rhyme

Ying away from yang
A whiz without a bang
Skiing without snow
A Frenchman sans chapeau

Happily Ever After

Like a jigsaw short a piece
Athens without Greece
A sculptor shy a chisel
Scotland wi' nae drizzle

The wind that blows no willow
The bed that has no pillow
Like a house without a roof
A dog who's lost his woof...

What I mean, my darling bride
Is, without you by my side
Like all these things and more
I'd be less
        Than what I was before.

The Owl and the Pussy-Cat
Edward Lear

I
The Owl and the Pussy-cat went to sea
  In a beautiful pea-green boat,
They took some honey, and plenty of money,
  Wrapped up in a five-pound note.
The Owl looked up to the stars above,
  And sang to a small guitar,
"O lovely Pussy! O Pussy, my love,
  What a beautiful Pussy you are,
    You are,
    You are!
What a beautiful Pussy you are!"

II
Pussy said to the Owl, "You elegant fowl!
  How charmingly sweet you sing!
O let us be married! too long we have tarried:
  But what shall we do for a ring?"
They sailed away, for a year and a day,
  To the land where the Bong-Tree grows
And there in a wood a Piggy-wig stood
  With a ring at the end of his nose,
    His nose,
    His nose,
  With a ring at the end of his nose.

III
"Dear Pig, are you willing to sell for one shilling
　　Your ring?" Said the Piggy, "I will."
So they took it away, and were married next day
　　By the Turkey who lives on the hill.
They dined on mince, and slices of quince,
　　Which they ate with a runcible spoon;
And hand in hand, on the edge of the sand,
　　They danced by the light of the moon,
　　　　　　The moon,
　　　　　　The moon,
They danced by the light of the moon.

READINGS

BIBLICAL

1 Corinthians 13

Though I speak with the tongues of men and of angels, but have not love, I have become sounding brass or a clanging cymbal.

And though I have the gift of prophecy, and understand all mysteries and all knowledge, and though I have all faith, so that I could remove mountains, but have not love, I am nothing.

And though I bestow all my goods to feed the poor, and though I give my body to be burned,[a] but have not love, it profits me nothing.

Love suffers long and is kind; love does not envy; love does not parade itself, is not puffed up; does not behave rudely, does not seek its own, is not provoked, thinks no evil; does not rejoice in iniquity, but rejoices in the truth; bears all things, believes all things, hopes all things, endures all things.

Love never fails. But whether there are prophecies, they will fail; whether there are tongues, they will cease; whether there is knowledge, it will vanish away. For we know in part and we prophesy in part. But when that which is perfect has come, then that which is in part will be done away.

When I was a child, I spoke as a child, I understood as a child, I thought as a child; but when I became a man, I put away childish things.

For now we see in a mirror, dimly, but then face to face. Now I know in part, but then I shall know just as I also am known. And now abide faith, hope, love, these three; but the greatest of these is love.

Genesis 2 (verses 18-24)

And the LORD God said, It is not good that man should be alone; I will make him an help meet for him.

And out of the ground the LORD God formed every beast of the field, and every fowl of the air; and brought them unto Adam to see what he would call them: and whatsoever Adam called every living creature, that was the name thereof.

And Adam gave names to all cattle, and to the fowl of the air, and to every beast of the field; but for Adam there was not found an help meet for him.

And the LORD God caused a deep sleep to fall upon Adam, and he slept: and he took one of his ribs, and closed up the flesh instead thereof;

And the rib, which the LORD God had taken from man, made he a woman, and brought her unto the man.

And Adam said, This is now bone of my bones, and flesh of my flesh: she shall be called Woman, because she was taken out of Man.

Therefore shall a man leave his father and his mother, and shall cleave unto his wife: and they shall be one flesh.

1 John 4 (verses 7-12)

Beloved, let us love one another: for love is of God; and every one that loveth is born of God, and knoweth God. He that loveth not knoweth not God; for God is love. In this was manifested the love of God toward us, because that God sent his only begotten Son into the world, that we might live through him. Herein is love, not that we loved God, but that he loved us, and sent his Son to be the propitiation for our sins. Beloved, if God so loved us, we ought also to love one another. No man hath seen God at any time. If we love one another, God dwelleth in us, and his love is perfected in us.

Ecclesiastes 4 (verses 9-12)

Two are better than one;
because they have a good reward for their labour.
For if they fall, the one will lift up his fellow:
but woe to him that is alone when he falleth;
for he hath not another to help him up.
Again, if two lie together, then they have heat:
but how can one be warm alone?
And if one prevail against him, two shall withstand him;
and a threefold cord is not quickly broken.

Song of Solomon 2 (verses 10-13)

My beloved speaks and says to me:
'Arise, my love, my fair one,
　and come away;
for now the winter is past,
　the rain is over and gone.

The flowers appear on the earth;
　the time of singing has come,
and the voice of the turtle-dove
　is heard in our land.

The fig tree puts forth its figs,
　and the vines are in blossom;
　they give forth fragrance.
Arise, my love, my fair one,
　and come away.

Song of Solomon 8 (verses 6-7)

Set me as a seal upon your heart,
   as a seal upon your arm;
for love is strong as death,
   passion fierce as the grave.
Its flashes are flashes of fire,
   a raging flame.

Many waters cannot quench love,
   neither can floods drown it.
If one offered for love
   all the wealth of one's house,
   it would be utterly scorned.

Mark 10 (verses 6-9)

But from the beginning of creation, "God made them male and female." "For this reason a man shall leave his father and mother and be joined to his wife, and the two shall become one flesh." So they are no longer two, but one flesh. Therefore what God has joined together, let no one separate.'

Mark 10 (verses 13-16)

People were bringing little children to him in order that he might touch them; and the disciples spoke sternly to them. But when Jesus saw this, he was indignant and said to them, 'Let the little children come to me; do not stop them; for it is to such as these that the kingdom of God belongs. Truly I tell you, whoever does not receive the kingdom of God as a little child will never enter it.' And he took them up in his arms, laid his hands on them, and blessed them.

John 2 (verses 1-11) – The Wedding at Cana

And the third day there was a marriage in Cana of Galilee; and the mother of Jesus was there:

And both Jesus was called, and his disciples, to the marriage. And when they wanted wine, the mother of Jesus said to him, 'They have no wine.'

Jesus said to her, 'Woman, what concern is that to you and me? My hour has not yet come.'

His mother said to the servants, 'Do whatever he tells you.'

And there were set there six waterpots of stone, after the manner of the purifying of the Jews, each holding twenty or thirty gallons.

Jesus said unto them, 'Fill the waterpots with water.' And they filled them up to the brim.

And he said to them, 'Draw out now, and bear unto the governor of the feast. And they bare it.'

When the ruler of the feast had tasted the water that was made wine, and knew not whence it was: (but the servants which drew the water knew;) the governor of the feast called the bridegroom,

And said unto him, Every man at the beginning sets forth good wine; and when said have well drunk, then that which is worse: but thou hast kept the good wine until now.'

This beginning of miracles did Jesus in Cana of Galilee, and manifested forth his glory; and his disciples believed on him.

Colossians 3 (verses 12-17)

As God's chosen ones, holy and beloved, clothe yourselves with compassion, kindness, humility, meekness, and patience. Bear with one another and, if anyone has a complaint against another, forgive each other; just as the Lord has forgiven you, so you also must forgive.

Above all, clothe yourselves with love, which binds everything together in perfect harmony. And let the peace of Christ rule in your hearts, to which indeed you were called in the one body. And be thankful.

Let the word of Christ dwell in you richly; teach and admonish one another in all wisdom; and with gratitude in your hearts sing psalms, hymns, and spiritual songs to God. And whatever you do, in word or deed, do everything in the name of the Lord Jesus, giving thanks to God the Father through him.

1 John 4 (verses 7-12)

Beloved, let us love one another, because love is from God; everyone who loves is born of God and knows God. Whoever does not love does not know God, for God is love. God's love was revealed among us in this way: God sent his only Son into the world so that we might live through him.

In this is love, not that we loved God but that he loved us and sent his Son to be the atoning sacrifice for our sins. Beloved, since God loved us so much, we also ought to love one another. No one has ever seen God; if we love one another, God lives in us, and his love is perfected in us.

NON-RELIGIOUS

These I Can Promise
Mark Twain

I cannot promise you a life of sunshine;
I cannot promise you riches, wealth or gold;
I cannot promise you an easy pathway
That leads away from change or growing old.
But I can promise all my heart's devotion;
A smile to chase away your tears of sorrow.
A love that's true and ever growing;
A hand to hold in your's through each tomorrow.

Paths and Journeys: Adapted from *Far from the Madding Crowd*
Thomas Hardy

We are all on our own paths, all on our own journeys. Sometimes the paths cross, and people arrive at the crossing points at the same time and meet each other. There are greetings, pleasantries are exchanged, and then they move on.

But then once in a while the pleasantries become more, friendship grows, deeper links are made, hands are joined and love flies.

The friendship has turned into love. Paths are joined, one path with two people walking it, both going in the same direction, and sharing each other's journeys.

Today <Name> and <Name> are joining their paths. They will now skip together in harmony and love, sharing joys and sorrows, hopes and fears, strengthening and upholding each other as they walk along side by side. At home by the fire, whenever I look up, there you will be. And whenever you look up, there I shall be.

Your Walled Garden
Author unknown

Your marriage should have within it a secret and protected space, open to you alone. Imagine it to be a walled garden, entered by a door to which you only hold the key.

Within this garden you will cease to be a mother, father, employee, homemaker or any other of the roles which you fulfil in daily life.

Here you can be yourselves, two people who love each other. Here you can concentrate on one another's needs. So take each other's hands and go forth to your garden. The time you spend together is not wasted but invested - invested in your future and nurture of your love.

A Celtic Blessing
Anonymous

Deep peace of the running wave to you,
Deep peace of the flowing air to you,
Deep peace of the quiet earth to you,
Deep peace of the shining stars to you,
Deep peace of the Son of Peace to you.
May the road rise to meet you;
May the wind be always at your back;
May the sun shine warm upon your face;
May the rains fall softly upon your fields.
Until we meet again,
May God hold you in the hollow of His hand.

The Blessing of the Apaches
Author unknown

Now you will feel no rain
For each of you will be shelter to the other.
Now you will feel no cold
For each of you will be warmth to the other.
Now there is no more loneliness for you
For each of you will be companion to the other.
Now you are two bodies
But there is only one life before you.
Go now to your dwelling place

Be at One with Each Other
George Eliot

What greater thing is there for two human souls than to feel that they are joined – to strengthen each other – to be at one with each other in silent unspeakable memories.

Marriage Advice
Jane Wells

Let your love be stronger than your hate or anger.
Learn the wisdom of compromise,
for it is better to bend a little than to break.
Believe the best rather than the worst.
People have a way of living up or down to your opinion of them.
Remember that true friendship is the basis for any lasting relationship.
The person you choose to marry is deserving of the courtesies
and kindnesses you bestow on your friends.

Please hand this down to your children and your children's children.

Never Marry But For Love
William Penn

Never marry but for love; but see that thou lovest what is
lovely.
He that minds a body and not a soul
has not the better part of that relationship,
and will consequently lack the noblest comfort of a married
life.

Between a man and his wife nothing ought to rule but love.
As love ought to bring them together,
so it is the best way to keep them well together.

A husband and wife that love one another
show their children that they should do so too.
Others visibly lose their authority in their families
by their contempt of one another,
and teach their children to be unnatural by their own
examples.

Let not enjoyment lessen, but augment, affection;
it being the basest of passions to like when we have not,
what we slight when we possess.

Here it is we ought to search out our pleasure,
where the field is large and full of variety, and of an
enduring nature;
sickness, poverty or disgrace being not able to shake it
because it is not under the moving influences of worldly
contingencies.

Nothing can be more entire and without reserve;
nothing more zealous, affectionate and sincere;
nothing more contented than such a couple,
nor greater temporal felicity than to be one of them.

(untitled)
Rumi

The minute I heard my first love story I started looking for you, not knowing how blind that was.

Lovers don't finally meet somewhere. They're in each other all along.

Extract from *The Velveteen Rabbit*
Margery Williams

'What is REAL?' asked the Rabbit one day, when they were lying side by side near the nursery fender, before Nana came to tidy the room. 'Does it mean having things that buzz inside you and a stick-out handle?' 'Real isn't how you are made,' said the Skin Horse. 'It's a thing that happens to you. When someone loves you for a long, long time, not just to play with, but REALLY loves you, then you become Real.' 'Does it hurt? Asked the Rabbit. 'Sometimes,' said the Skin Horse, for he was always truthful. 'When you are Real you don't mind being hurt.' 'Does it happen all at once, like being wound up,' he asked, 'or bit by bit?' ' It doesn't happen all at once,' said the Skin Horse. 'You become. It takes a long time. That's why it doesn't happen often to people who break easily, or have sharp edges, or who have to be carefully kept. Generally, by the time you are Real, most of your hair has been loved off, and your eyes drop out and you get loose in your joints and very shabby. But these things don't matter at all, because once you are Real you can't be ugly, except to people who don't understand.' 'I suppose you are real?' said the Rabbit. And then he wished he had not said it, for he thought the Skin Horse only smiled. 'Someone made me Real,' he said. 'That was a great many years ago; but once you are Real you can't become unreal again. It lasts for always.'

About the Editor

Richard Happer is the author of over 15 books, most of which have some love in them.

His novel, *The Hills Are Stuffed With Swedish Girls*, is very definitely about love. Well, about how men sometimes mistake love for lust...

CPSIA information can be obtained
at www.ICGtesting.com
Printed in the USA
LVOW12s0127280218
568151LV00005B/226/P